Microscopic Life
in your
Body

BRIAN WARD

W
FRANKLIN WATTS
LONDON · SYDNEY

Contents and definitions

4 Living with microbes

6 'Good' microbes

8 The immune system

10 Bigger creatures

Bacteria

Bacteria are tiny organisms, far too small to be seen without a microscope. They live just about everywhere. Bacteria may be rounded, threadlike or rod-shaped, and some of them can creep about, using waving threads called flagella. Some bacteria need oxygen to live, while others are killed by the oxygen in the air.

Viruses

Viruses are even tinier than bacteria. Unlike many bacteria, viruses need to infect a living cell if they are to grow and reproduce. They take over the whole of the workings of the cell and turn it into a virus factory. This usually kills the cell as the new viruses are released.

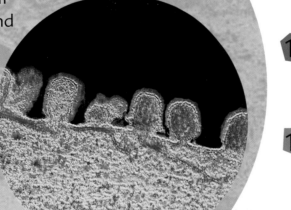

12 Spreading diseases

14 An upset stomach

16 Bacterial attack

18 Tooth attack

20 Virus attack

22 Skin microbes

24 Hot bugs

26 Keeping clean

Fungi

Fungi are small organisms that mostly feed on dead and decaying material. Some small fungi called yeasts can cause disease when they grow on moist parts of the body surface, such as between your toes.

Tiny animals

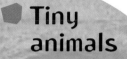

Tiny animal-like microbes called Protista cause serious diseases such as malaria in some tropical parts of the world.

Mites and lice

Large numbers of tiny eight-legged, spider-like creatures called mites live on your body and in your bed, feeding on small pieces of skin. Other mites burrow into your skin. Small flat insects called lice can live on your skin, feeding on your blood.

28 Fighting back

30 Glossary

31 Further information

32 Index

Living with microbes

You can not get away from microbes. With every breath you take, you breathe in millions of them.

How do microbes get inside you?

Microbes are microscopic living things. Most of these tiny organisms that you breathe in, you breathe out again. Those that stay in are quickly attacked by your body, so they hardly ever do any harm. You also swallow millions of bugs with every mouthful of food or drink, although most of these are killed by the strong acid in your stomach. Everything you touch is covered in bacteria, which you transfer to your mouth from your fingers when you eat, usually without doing any harm.

◄

Each mouthful of food is loaded with bacteria and viruses.

How big are cells?

Put some sticky tape on your wrist. Rip it off quickly and place it under a microscope. You should be able to see some dead skin cells on it.

Friendly microbes

Millions more harmless bacteria live on the surface of your skin, but most of the 'good' bacteria live in your gut, or intestines, where they help to keep you healthy. Most microbes can live on and in us without causing any harm at all. In fact, we need some of them to help keep us healthy, and at least 95% of them are harmless. Disease is only caused when the microbes grow and increase in numbers faster than the body can kill them.

MICRO FACTS

The microbe farm

Your body is made up of millions and millions of cells — but for every one of your body cells there are 19 bacteria cells living in your body. In addition, there are all of the viruses lurking inside your body cells, and other organisms living on your skin. Your body is a microbe farm!

▼ *Your gut is home to millions of bacteria which help us digest our food.*

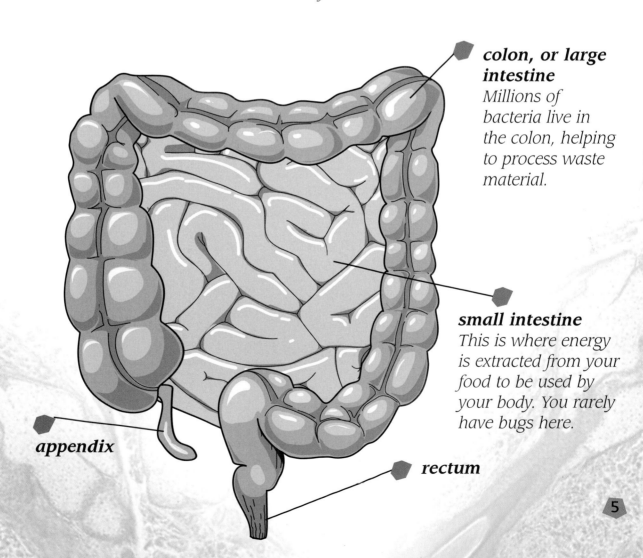

colon, or large intestine
Millions of bacteria live in the colon, helping to process waste material.

small intestine
This is where energy is extracted from your food to be used by your body. You rarely have bugs here.

appendix

rectum

'Good' microbes

The bugs that live in your colon are 'good' bugs because they help to break down your food.

How do bacteria help with digestion?

Food is digested in your intestines. It is broken down by substances called enzymes, so it can be absorbed and used by the body. Some food cannot be digested in this way. The bacteria in your colon helps to break down these indigestible food parts, so your body can use it properly. The bacteria use some of the food for themselves, but they also make other useful food substances that we can use. Some vitamins are produced in the colon by bacteria.

Eating 'good' bugs

Many of these 'good' bacteria are like those that grow in milk and make it sour. Some people like to eat 'live' yoghurt, which contains huge numbers of these bacteria, to add to the numbers in their colon.

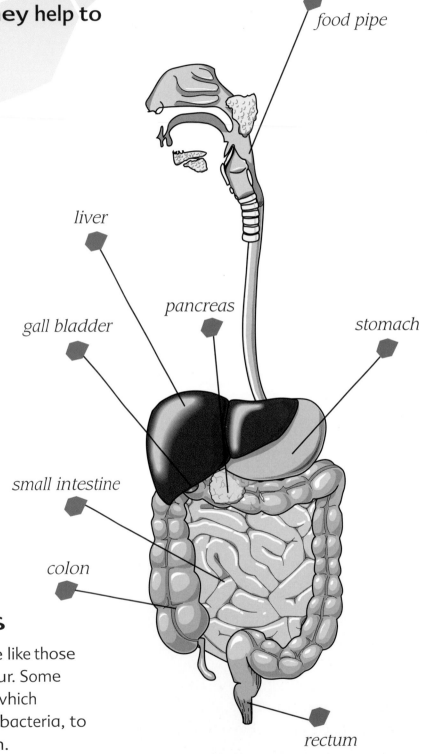

food pipe

liver

pancreas

gall bladder

stomach

small intestine

colon

rectum

MICRO FACTS

Some amazing facts about the bacteria living inside you

- You have about 1 kg of bacteria in your colon.
- Every gram of faeces (or poo) contains 100,000 million bacteria.
- Every day, people on Earth produce more than 5 billion kg of faeces. Just think about how many bacteria that means!

Smelly microbes...

One sign of the 'good' bacteria in your colon is farting! The bacteria working away in your colon produce gas that escapes from the body as a belch or fart. Most people fart 10 to 15 times each day (not always quietly). Even this is nothing compared to cows, who fart so much of a gas called methane that some scientists think they may be helping to make the whole surface of the Earth heat up.

...and skinny microbes

'Good' or harmless microbes also live in huge numbers on your skin, feeding on the oily sebum produced from the tiny pits or follicles where hairs grow. Their great numbers crowd out harmful bacteria so they cannot grow and cause skin diseases.

TRY IT YOURSELF

How hairy are you?

Use a hand magnifier to study your own skin. How many hair follicles are there on the back of your hand? Ask a friend if you can study their face. Imagine all the 'good' bacteria living in the follicles you can see.

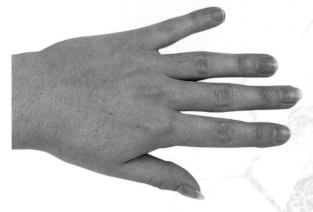

The immune system

If we are surrounded by billions of bugs waiting to feed on our bodies, why aren't we ill all the time?

Germs have markers called antigens on their surface. Each lymphocyte recognises a particular antigen, like a key fits a lock.

bacterium

antigen (or marker)

lymphocytes

lymphocyte locks on to marker

lymphocyte multiplies rapidly

memory cell (remembers invader's antigens)

When the lymphocyte recognises a germ, it divides to produce two types of cells: memory cells that memorise the antigen, and plasma cells that release antibodies. Antibodies disable the germ.

antibody

plasma cell (produces antibodies)

Identifying the enemy

Threatened every day by billions of germs, your body has a very good defence: the immune system. Huge numbers of special white blood cells, called lymphocytes, are carried around your body in the blood, ready to find an invading microbe germ. As soon as lymphocytes touch an unfamiliar cell or substance, they begin to produce chemicals called antibodies which attack the invaders, killing or damaging them. The lymphocytes also make memory cells so the body recognises the germ in the future. The cells then 'learn' how to make a new antibody, which over a few days builds up to overcome the invading microbes.

Resisting infection

Once they have made an antibody that will kill a particular microbe, the lymphocytes remember how to do it. If the same microbe enters the body some time later, they respond by producing the proper antibody very quickly, so the infection never has the chance to develop properly. This is called immunity. You catch most diseases only once, because after that you are fully immune. However, you may still have lots of colds, because colds can be caused by hundreds of different types of virus which all cause similar coughs and sneezes. You would have to become immune to all of them to prevent all colds.

Coughs and sneezes do spread diseases, ▶
so cover your mouth to avoid infecting
other people.

Virus in disguise

The flu or influenza virus, which is very different from the cold virus, often causes epidemics, when lots of people become ill. The virus changes slightly each year, so even if you have had the disease before, your body may not recognise the slightly altered virus and it will not be able to make an antibody right away. The flu virus is very strange because it seems to live naturally in ducks and pigs in China, and a different type of flu spreads from them to humans every few years.

Bigger creatures

Here's a creepy thought — there are lots of tiny creatures with **legs** walking about on you! Most of these are harmless.

● Creatures in your skin

You may be carrying around some tiny creatures called mites, which are about 0.4 mm long. They live in the pores and hair follicles in your face, and especially in the roots of your eyelashes. These little creatures feed on oil and dead skin cells, and though they look nasty they are quite harmless.

▶ *Tiny mites may be living in the pores of your face, although they do not do any harm.*

MICRO FACTS

Burrowing mites

One type of mite can cause unpleasant skin infections, burrowing through the skin and causing itchy red tracks. This condition is called scabies and it sometimes affects people who do not take care to clean themselves properly. Scabies is spread by touching an infected person, or sometimes by touching a pet suffering from a skin condition called mange.

Mites in the bed

Some other types of mite, called dust mites, walk around on your skin feeding on loose flakes of dead skin. These mites are too small to see, but there can be millions of them in your bed or your pillow, feeding on bits of shed skin. Many more of them live in the carpet. Mites are related to spiders, but they have much shorter legs. These mites are harmless, although their droppings make some people sneeze or wheeze. This is a common allergy, and people who suffer from it use special pillows and mattress covers.

Your bed may contain millions of microscopic mites, feeding on bits of shed skin.

What is a nit?

Lice also live on your skin, in the hair, where they feed on blood. They are small, flat insects that are difficult to see as they cling to a hair. Young lice are completely transparent. As they grow they become the colour of the hair they live in. Usually they are only identified when their egg sacs, called nits, are seen in the hair. These are yellowish objects like tiny grains of rice. Lice and nits are spread by contact with an infected person, and the condition is very common among groups of children who play together. The easiest way to get rid of lice and nits is to comb hair thoroughly with a fine-toothed comb.

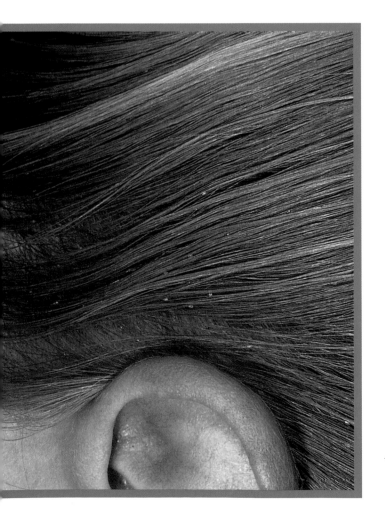

Nits are the egg sacs of mites, which live in the hair and suck blood.

11

Spreading diseases

Microbes are very resourceful and can get into our bodies in several different ways.

Breathing in

The commonest way to become infected is breathing in from the air, after someone coughs or sneezes. Coughing and sneezing shoot out millions of bacteria or viruses from people's lungs. Colds and flu are the most common infections spread in this way. Hundreds of different viruses can cause the symptoms of a cold.

◀

Every time you sneeze you shoot a stream of infected water drops across the room.

A sneeze spreads disease

A sneeze can blast a stream of water droplets for 2 metres, and if you have a cold or chest infection, each tiny droplet may contain millions of microbes, ready to be breathed in by someone else. This is why it is hygienic as well as polite to put your hand over your mouth when you cough or sneeze.

Measure 2 metres from your mouth to see how far your sneeze can travel!

Microbes in your mouth

More than 500 different types of bacteria live in your mouth! Most are harmless, but they can be transferred to another person by kissing, sharing a toothbrush or drinking from an unwashed glass or cup. Cold sores are also spread by this sort of contact, and so is a virus infection called glandular fever, which often affects older children and students.

People can be catching!

Many people become infectious before they show any signs of illness, which is why childhood diseases such as mumps and chickenpox spread so quickly through groups of children.

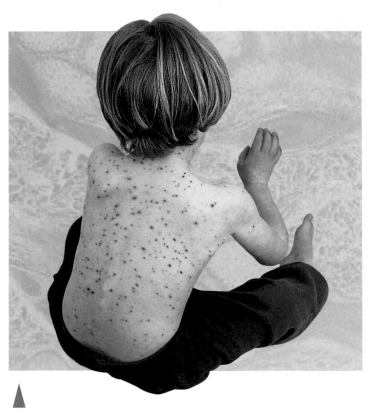

Spots and rashes like this mean that someone is infected with viruses or bacteria.

MICRO FACTS

Pet threat

Believe it or not, more than 100 types of microbe can be spread by the saliva in the mouths of cats and dogs. Never let pets lick your face or share your food, as this will leave lots of bacteria around your mouth. *Salmonella* bacteria are often found in pet birds and especially in reptiles. They are also found in uncooked eggs and chicken meat. The animals are not usually affected by the bacteria, but they can cause very unpleasant stomach upsets when they get into humans. Wash your hands carefully after handling animals, and make sure you always cook your food thoroughly to kill any bacteria.

An upset stomach

Why is it that when you travel abroad on holiday you often get diarrhoea?

Many people pick up gut infections on holiday. ▼

Traveller's tummy

You have billions of bacteria in your gut, and over the years you have got used to them. The different types of microbes all live together happily, helping you to digest your food. Then you go away on holiday and eat food or drink water that contains some different microbes that live in the local people. Usually this happens because faeces are not treated properly in a sewage works, so the microbes they contain pass into the drinking water, and then into you. Once the new type of bacteria enter your system from your food or drink, they begin to grow, upsetting the balance of the bacteria already there. This is what causes diarrhoea and stomach pains, and it can take a few days before your own bacteria overcome the new ones.

Mucky food

Even worse stomach upsets can be caused if food is not treated hygienically or cooked thoroughly, giving the dangerous bacteria the chance to multiply before it is eaten. This can happen if someone handling food has not washed their hands properly after using the toilet. Flies carry infection, too, on their feet. If they walk in your food, they spread bacteria, so you must take care to cover food that is left in the open.

Flies walking in your food ▶ often spread bacteria and viruses that cause diarrhoea.

MICRO FACTS

What is food poisoning?

Food poisoning happens when food has not been handled hygienically, enabling bacteria to grow and sometimes produce poisons called toxins. Common foods such as chicken and eggs often cause a form of food poisoning called salmonellosis, which can make you very ill. Another very dangerous form of food poisoning is caused by bacteria related to the ones living in your gut, called *E. coli*, which can lead to serious disease outbreaks.

Bacterial attack

Usually it takes a large number of bacteria to start an infection that will make you ill. Ordinarily, the body can overcome small numbers of bacteria very quickly, but if bacteria get into the body in huge numbers they may cause serious harm.

Where do bacteria live?

Most bacteria live and grow in their favourite part of the body. *Streptococci* bacteria are a common cause of sore throats and tonsillitis. They live in the tissues, feeding on them and the liquid around the cells, and as they grow and divide, they produce poisonous waste materials called toxins. These poisons are carried round the body in the blood, making you feel hot and achy.

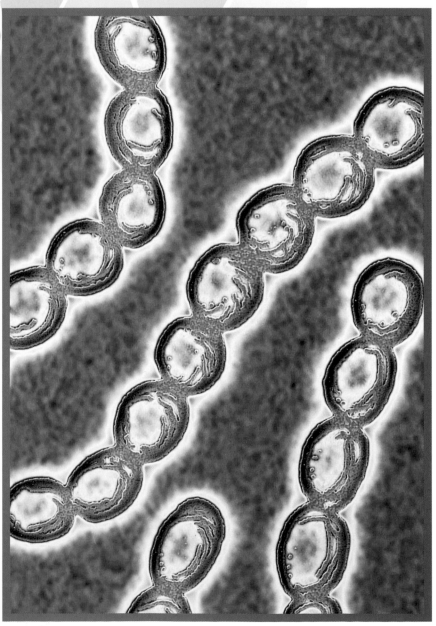

The Streptococci bacteria that often cause sore throats may grow in long chains.

Meningitis

Meningitis is a very serious disease that can be caused by bacteria infecting the skin-like covering of the brain, where it causes a very bad headache and a high temperature. Other types of meningitis are caused by viruses.

Have i caught something?

After you have been exposed to an infection, you do not become ill immediately, if at all. The period of time between catching an infection and becoming ill is called the 'incubation period'. Usually, more than two weeks can pass after you have been infected before signs of the illness appear:

Chickenpox	14-16 days
Mumps	14-24 days
Rubella (German measles)	14-21 days

How long will i be ill?

Some infections are acute. This means that they come on suddenly and clear up quite quickly. Most sore throats are infections of this type. A 'chronic' infection lasts much longer. One example of a chronic infection is the disease tuberculosis (TB). The TB bacteria are breathed into the lungs and often remain there for years without changing very much. Then they can suddenly start growing again and cause very serious disease.

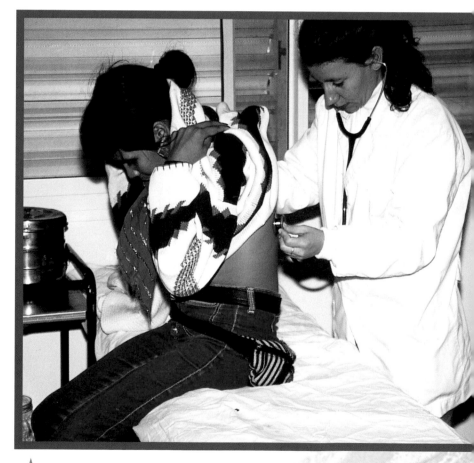

A doctor uses a stethoscope to hear the wheezing in your lungs caused by infection.

Tooth attack

Like the rest of your body, your mouth is warm and wet. This habitat provides the ideal conditions for bacteria to grow in. Some mouth bacteria cause tooth decay and cavities (holes), and may even cause the loss of a tooth.

Bacteria in the mouth

Most of the bacteria in your mouth cause no problems, but there is one type called *Streptococcus mutans* ('Strep' for short) that causes tooth decay. Strep bacteria are tiny round organisms that feed on the sugar in your food and produce a waste material called lactic acid. This acid eats into the hard enamel surface of the tooth, softening it and causing a cavity that lets other dangerous bacteria get inside and do more damage. Drinking fizzy drinks often makes the damage worse, because they also contain acid.

Bacteria in plaque attack a tooth that has had its enamel damaged by acid.

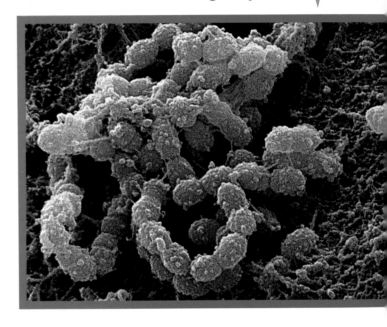

The threat from sugar

When you eat sweets, the sugar they contain is just what these Strep bacteria need to grow and cause damage. They form a slimy layer of bacteria over your teeth, called plaque. You can feel this with your tongue after you have been eating sweet foods, and it needs to be removed quickly by brushing your teeth thoroughly. People who do not eat sweet things have 90% fewer cavities!

Losing your teeth

As well as causing cavities, a layer of plaque on the teeth can do lots more damage if it is not removed properly. It gradually hardens into a stony brown layer around the bottom of the tooth, and this makes the gums sore. Then more harmful bacteria get into the base of the tooth and may cause so much damage that eventually the tooth has to be taken out.

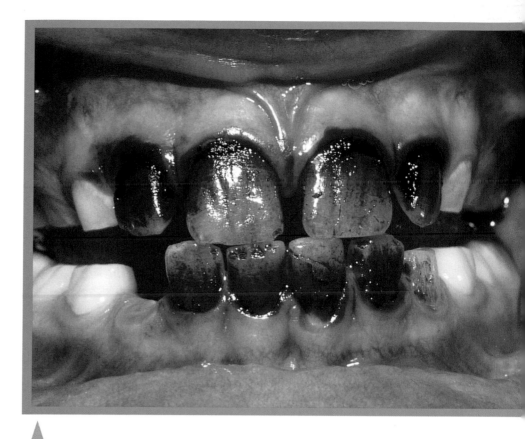

Bacteria and the plaque they cause can damage teeth so much that they eventually have to be removed.

TRY IT YOURSELF

See how acid attacks teeth!

If you have a tooth that the tooth fairy missed taking away, drop it into a clear plastic bottle containing a fizzy drink (check the label to see that the drink contains citric or phosphoric acid). If you cannot find a tooth, use a piece of chicken bone, which is similar to tooth enamel. Stand it in a safe place, then after a couple of weeks check to see what has happened to the tooth or piece of bone. Then think about what could be happening in your own mouth! When you have finished with it, throw everything away carefully.

Virus attack

Viruses cause most of the common illnesses of children. Mumps, rubella and chickenpox are all caused by virus infections. They are all highly contagious, causing outbreaks of disease that affect large groups of children.

Virus takeover

Viruses have a peculiar way of life. Some experts even think that they are not alive at all because they cannot grow or reproduce on their own — to do so they have to enter the cells of a living organism that can. When viruses enter the body they are normally attacked by the immune system, but if some of them escape, they can get into body cells.

Each of our cells contains a command centre called the nucleus, which gives instructions to the cell about what it should do. The virus enters this nucleus and takes over, giving its own instructions to make huge numbers of new viruses. Eventually these tiny particles burst out of the cell and float away to infect other healthy cells.

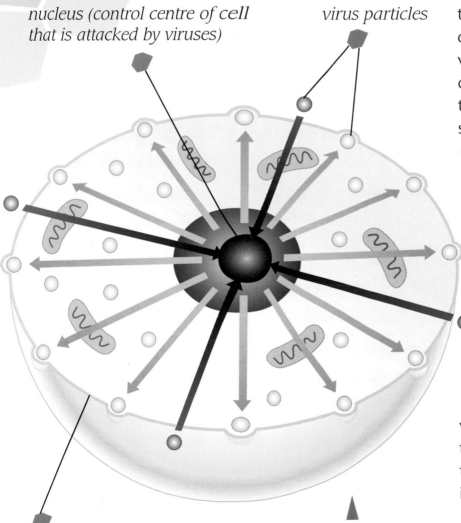

nucleus (control centre of cell that is attacked by viruses)

virus particles

cell membrane

A diagram of a cell being attacked by a virus. The virus particles multiply hugely in the nucleus and then bud off from the cell wall to infect other cells.

Sneaky viruses

While these viruses are in the cell, the body's defences cannot find them. The viruses are only attacked when they burst out. It is the waste materials, or poisons, that are released when the viruses burst out from cells that cause the typical aching feeling that you have with a cold or other virus infection. Illnesses caused by viruses are usually 'acute' infections that clear up quite quickly. However, they may leave you feeling very wobbly for a while, and you are likely to catch some other infection while you are weakened.

Tiny flu virus particles are budded off from the surface of an infected cell to spread the infection to other cells. ▼

MICRO FACTS

What causes AIDS?

HIV is the virus associated with the serious disease AIDS. It is very unusual because it infects and damages the cells of the immune system that normally fight infections, so the body has no effective way to defend itself. HIV is also unusual because it takes a long time after infection for its effects to appear. The virus itself does not necessarily lead to AIDS, but lots of infections that would normally be prevented by the immune system are able to cause immense damage.

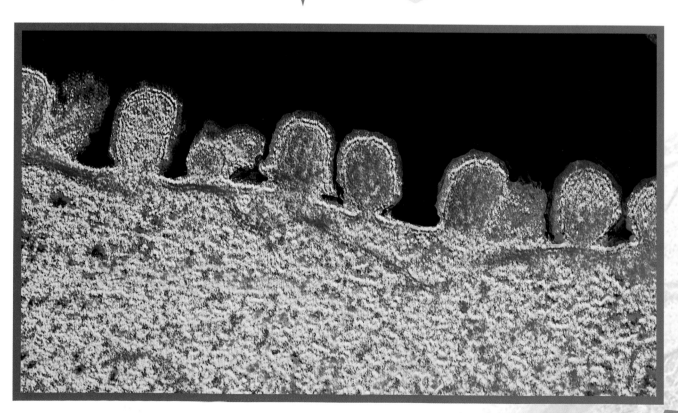

Skin microbes

You are often aware when microbes infect your skin and cause disease because you can see the spots and pimples that they produce.

How are spots caused?

Large numbers of bacteria live in the hair follicles on your skin. The oily substance called sebum, produced in the root of hairs, is an ideal food for them. If the follicle becomes blocked, the oily sebum collects and the trapped bacteria multiply, causing a red spot or pimple. Sometimes the bacteria move deeper into the skin and attack the tissues, causing a boil. The yellowish pus in a boil is the remains of dead bacteria and the body cells attacking them.

Oily sebum trapped in skin follicles encourages the growth of bacteria that cause spots and pimples.

Cold sores

Viruses often attack the skin around your lips, causing painful cold sores. Once you have been infected with the cold sore virus, it will get inside the cells, where it stays until you are weakened by tiredness or some other infection. Then it breaks out and produces cold sores, which usually come back every time you feel tired and worn out.

Foot fungus

Athlete's Foot is an infection caused by a tiny fungus that feeds on skin cells, usually between your toes. The skin becomes sore and peels, and sometimes even toe nails become infected. Athlete's Foot is often caught at swimming pools as it can easily survive in the warm, wet habitat. The infection can be treated with medicines that you can buy in pharmacies.

Tiny threads of fungus cause Athlete's Foot. They can also cause skin infections in other parts of the body. ►

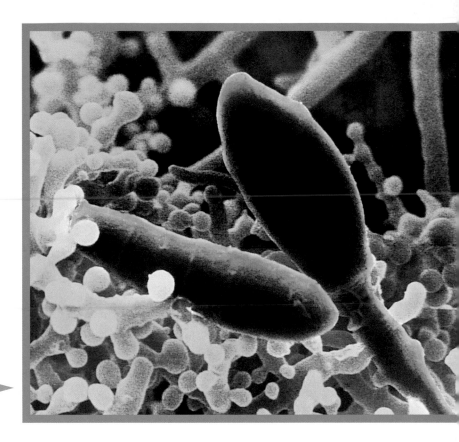

Warts and verrucas

Warts are caused by a virus. The cells it infects divide and grow, producing a lump on the skin, usually on your hands. Another form of wart called a verruca grows on the sole of your foot, but the lump grows inwards, so it is uncomfortable to walk on it. The verruca virus, like Athlete's Foot, thrives in swimming pools and changing rooms.

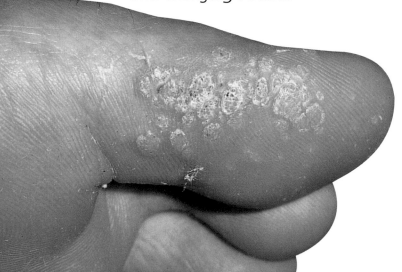

MICRO FACTS

What's in a wart?

The outer layer of the skin is made of lots of cells that divide very quickly. The skin cells on the surface die and flake off as new cells grow beneath them. The wart virus infects these dividing cells and makes them divide even more quickly. They build up into a lump, or wart, because they grow faster than they die off.

Hot bugs

Microbes can cause very serious diseases in tropical parts of the world, and sometimes in other countries, too. These microbes are known as 'hot bugs'.

Burying victims of the 'Black Death' or plague – a medieval 'hot bug'.

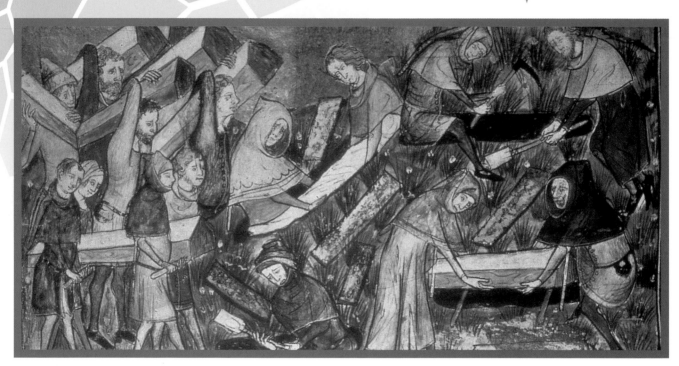

MICRO FACTS

The Black Death

Around 600 years ago, one in every three people in Europe was killed by the Black Death, or plague. This was a disease of rats caused by bacteria. People were infected in two ways: firstly, fleas living on the rats would bite them and pick up the bacteria. Then they would bite someone and transfer the bacteria from the rat to the person. Secondly, the disease spread through the air when infected people coughed up the bacteria from their lungs. This bacteria would then be breathed in by someone else and infect them. In those days people did not know about micro-organisms or how they spread disease. Plague moved across Europe in waves of disease but it gradually became less serious. It now very rarely causes disease and can be treated with antibiotics (see page 29).

Killing off the virus

Smallpox was a killer disease that existed for thousands of years. It is a virus that causes masses of sores over the skin, and killed many of the people that it infected. Smallpox is the only human disease that has ever been wiped out in nature, due to vaccination (see page 28) of all the people living in the areas where it existed. Some of the virus is still kept in laboratories.

These tiny yellow ▶ *microbes are malaria parasites entering red blood cells. The cells die making the infected people very ill.*

Mosquito threat

Malaria is a common disease in tropical countries that is spread by the bite of an infected mosquito. It is caused by tiny microbes called *Plasmodium*, which are neither bacteria nor viruses, but belong to a separate group of microbes called Protista. Malaria causes very high temperatures and affects millions of people living in the tropics. Many children in Africa are killed by this disease.

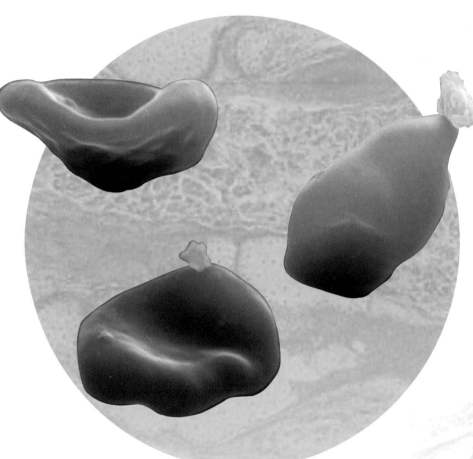

New threats

Many of the most dangerous tropical diseases are animal infections that can also attack people. Some of these diseases cause outbreaks when people come into contact with the animals as they move into new living areas. Ebola fever is one such killer disease, caused by a virus. It attacks people in the jungles of parts of Africa, though no one knows yet which animal it usually affects. HIV (the virus causing the condition called AIDS) is also thought to have arisen in this way, probably in apes or monkeys in Africa, but it has now spread around the world. It can only be caught by contact with the body fluids, such as blood, of an infected person.

Keeping clean

There are lots of ways to avoid infection with microbes, and also to prevent passing them on to other people.

Wash your hands!

Washing hands after using the toilet and before eating is the most important single thing you can do to avoid becoming infected by the microbes that are all around you. Rinsing your hands is not enough — you need to give them a good scrubbing with soap and water, paying special attention to cleaning under your nails where dirt and microbes can gather. You must also be very careful to clean yourself properly after using the toilet.

Scrub your hands after using the toilet, when preparing food and before eating.

Don't forget to wash your hands thoroughly after helping to change a baby's nappy, handling rubbish in the dustbin, handling raw meat or playing with your pets. All of these activities can be the cause of infection.

Many modern soaps have an antibacterial agent added.

🔷 Skin care

Showering and bathing help keep you clean by reducing the numbers of bacteria on the surface of your skin. Frequent and thorough washing with soap will help keep your skin clear of spots, too, though sometimes these cannot be avoided, especially in teenagers. Do not use disinfectants or medicated soaps on your face. These will remove too much of the skin's natural protective oils — and the harmless bacteria that crowd out the ones causing the spots.

Sebum soon makes your hair look greasy and straggly if you do not wash it regularly.

MICRO FACTS

Pooh! Smelly feet!

Did you know that smelly feet and armpits are caused by bacteria feeding on the oily sebum in your hair follicles? Frequent washing removes the sebum so the bacteria have nothing to feed on, and you will not smell sweaty. Socks and trainers smell bad for just the same reason. Wash them often!

Fighting back

Our bodies can usually fight infection, but sometimes they need some help. We can do this by encouraging the body to strengthen its defences, or by taking drugs to kill harmful bacteria.

⬡ What is vaccination?

One way to prevent disease caused by bacteria or viruses is to kill them as soon as they enter the body. Your body can be encouraged to fight back quickly by a process called vaccination. Vaccines are usually injected, or sometimes swallowed, like the polio vaccine children are given, before a person is exposed to infections. The vaccines contain weak or harmless microbes, dead microbes or, sometimes, just some important parts of the microbes. The body's immune system recognises the 'invaders' and reacts as though they were a real threat to health, manufacturing protective antibodies. When the real invaders strike, the antibodies can now be produced very quickly, preventing an infection from developing. Vaccination is valuable because it works to protect you against attack from both bacteria and viruses.

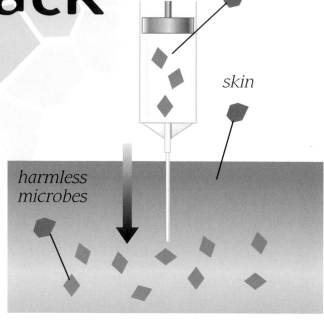

1. A person is injected with harmless microbes or bits of microbes that do not cause the disease.

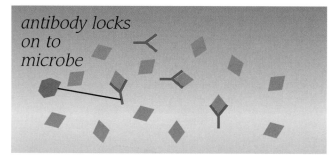

2. Although the microbial material is harmless, the body still recognises it and makes antibodies against it.

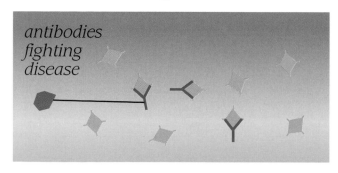

3. If the body is invaded by the real microbes, the immune system responds immediately with huge numbers of antibodies to destroy the disease.

Antibiotics to kill bacteria

Some natural substances fight bacteria (but not viruses) by interfering with the way that they reproduce. These substances are called antibiotics. They weaken the bacteria, which are then quickly killed by the body's own defences. Antibiotics can only treat an infection once it has appeared so, unlike vaccines, they cannot be used to prevent infection. They do not kill viruses so they do not help if you have a cold or the flu.

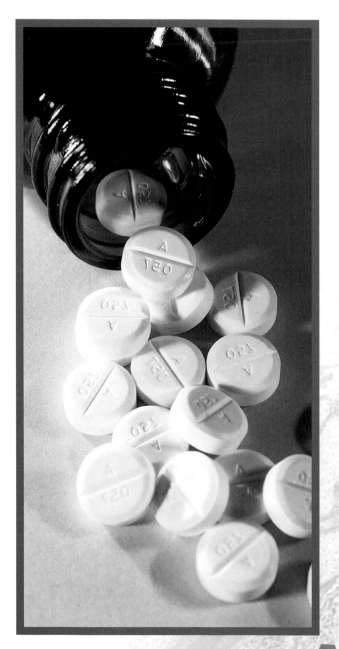

Glossary

AIDS: Acquired Immune Deficiency Syndrome; a serious disease spread by contact with body fluids from an infected person.

Antibiotic: Drug that attacks bacteria and sometimes other microbes.

Antibody: Substance produced in the body to fight invading microbes or other substances that enter the blood system.

Bacteria: Tiny single-celled microbes that live nearly everywhere, including people's bodies, food and homes. Some bacteria can be 'good', for example helping people to digest food. Other bacteria can be 'bad', because they cause diseases.

Citric acid: Sharp-tasting substance found in fruit and often added to fizzy drinks. It can be prepared by fermentation.

Decay: Process of breakdown of dead material by microbes.

Diarrhoea: Condition that may be caused by infection, in which food passes very quickly through the digestive system.

Ebola: A very dangerous, but rare, disease first found in Africa. It is caused by a virus, but no one knows how it spreads.

Enamel: The hard, shiny surface layer of the teeth.

Faeces: Solid waste that remains after food is digested.

Flagella: Thin, hair-like strands found on some bacteria and other microbes. They may allow the microbe to move about.

Flea: Tiny jumping insect, mostly found on cats, which bite and feed on their blood. They also bite people.

Follicle: The tiny socket in the skin from which a hair grows.

Fungus: Organism that breaks down dead material and sometimes also causes diseases. Most fungi are microscopic; others are large, like mushrooms.

Habitat: The place where organisms live.

HIV: Human Immune deficiency Virus; the virus that causes AIDS.

Hygiene: Measures to control the level of microbes around us such as washing hands and cleaning kitchen work surfaces.

Immunity: When the body can fight off microbes having been infected once before.

Lactic acid: Sour-tasting substance produced when bacteria cause milk to 'go off'.

Lice: Tiny flat insects that cling to hair, feeding on blood.

Lymphocytes: Body cells that fight infection.

Malaria: Tropical disease caused by tiny animal-like parasites, injected into the body by the bite of a mosquito.

Microbe: An organism that is so small it can only be seen with the aid of a microscope.

Mite: Tiny spider-like animal that feeds on skin flakes, food debris or sometimes on people.

Nits: The cream-coloured eggs of head lice.

Oxygen: Colourless gas in the air we breathe.

Parasite: An animal or other living organisms that feeds on another form of life.

Plaque: Slimy layer of bacteria covering the teeth.

Protista: Tiny animal-like organisms.

Pus: Yellowish remains of dead bacteria and body cells that fight infection.

Salmonellosis: Disease caused by eating food that has been contaminated by large numbers of *Salmonella* bacteria.

Scabies: Itchy skin disease caused by mites that burrow under the skin surface.

Sebum: Oily liquid produced from hair follicles, helping to keep the skin flexible.

Smallpox: Very dangerous disease caused by a virus, but now extinct in nature because of vaccination programmes.

Strep: Abbreviation for bacteria called *Streptococcus.*

Tonsillitis: Painful infection of the tonsils, small fleshy patches in the back of the throat.

Toxin: Poisonous substance produced by some types of bacteria.

Tuberculosis (TB): A serious disease caused by bacteria, which mostly attacks the lungs. It can be prevented by vaccination.

Vaccination: Process that produces immunity to an infection. Vaccines may be taken by mouth or injected. They contain dead or harmless microbes, or parts of them, and they cause the body to react by producing antibodies.

Verruca: Virus infection of the skin on the sole of the foot.

Virus: Very simple organism that can only grow and reproduce inside a living cell. All viruses are parasites.

Wart: Virus infection of the skin, producing a small lump.

Further information

The following websites contain lots of useful information about microbes and their effects on the body:

Microbe Zoo: **http://commtechlab.msu. edu/sites/dlc-me/zoo**

Microbe World: **http://www. microbeworld.org**

Microbiology on-line: **http://www.microbiology online.org.uk/wom.htm**

Head lice: **http://hcd2.bupa. co.uk/fact_sheets/Mosby_ factsheets/head_lice.html**

Eyelash mites: **http://geocities. com/thesciencefiles/eyelash/ creatures.html**

Microbes in sickness and in health: **http://www.niaid.nih. gov/publications/microbes.htm**

Stalking the mysterious microbe: **http://www. microbe.org**

Scabies: **http://www.aad. org/pamphlets/Scabies.html**

index

acids 4, 18, 19
AIDS 21, 25
allergy 11
antibody 8, 9
antigen 8

bacteria 2, 4, 5, 6, 7, 12, 13, 14, 15, 16–17, 18, 19, 22, 24, 27
blood 3, 8, 11, 16, 25

cavity 18, 19
cell 2, 4, 8, 10, 20, 21, 22, 23, 25
colds 9, 12, 21
colon 5, 6

decay 3, 18
diarrhoea 14
digestive system 5, 6
disease 3, 5, 7, 9, 13, 15, 17, 20, 24, 25

E.coli 15
enamel 18, 19
enzyme 5, 6

faeces 7, 14
flagella 2

flies 15
flu 9, 12
follicle 7, 10, 22, 27
food 4, 14, 15, 26
food poisoning 15
fungus 3, 23

germ 8
gut 5, 14

HIV 21, 25
hygiene 14, 15, 26–27

immune system 8–9, 20, 21
incubation period 17
infection 10, 13, 17, 21, 22, 23, 25, 26
intestine 5, 6

lice 3, 11
lung 4, 17, 24
lymphocyte 8, 9

malaria 3, 25
meningitis 16
microbe 3, 4–5, 6–7, 8, 9, 12, 13, 14, 15, 22–23, 24, 25, 26
mite 3, 10–11

nit 11

oxygen 2

plaque 18, 19
pore 10
Protista 3, 25

Salmonella 13
sebum 6, 22, 27
skin 3, 4, 5, 7, 10, 11, 22–23, 25, 27
smallpox 25
sneezing 9, 12
spots 13, 22, 27
stomach upset 13, 14–15
Streptococci 16
sugar 18

tooth 18–19
toxin 15, 16
tuberculosis (TB) 17

vaccination 25, 28
virus 2, 4, 9, 10, 12, 13, 16, 20–21, 25
virus particle 20, 21

yeast 3

This edition 2005
Franklin Watts
96 Leonard Street
LONDON EC2A 4XD

Franklin Watts Australia
Level 17/207 Kent Street
Sydney NSW 2000

© 2003 Franklin Watts

A CIP catalogue record for this book is available from the British Library

ISBN: 0 7496 6334 0
Dewey Number: 616'.01
Printed in China

Editor: Kate Banham
Designer: Joelle Wheelwright
Art direction: Peter Scoulding
Illustrations: David Graham
Picture research: Diana Morris
Educational consultant: Dot Jackson

Acknowledgements

The publishers would like to thank the following for permission to reproduce photographs in this book:

Anthony Bannister/Corbis: 15t. Mark Clarke/SPL: 13b. CNRI/SPL: 2b, 21. A.Crump, TDR, WHO/SPL: 17. Dennis Degnan/Corbis: 11t. Eye of Science/SPL: 3cl, 25. E. Guelio/CNRI/SPL: fr cover cl, b cover cr, 3tr, 23t. Dr. Chris Hale/SPL: 11b. Dr. P. Marazzi/SPL: 23. Matt Meadows, Peter Arnold Inc./SPL: 12. Cordelia Molloy/SPL: 29. Alfred Pasieka/SPL: fr cover tr, b cover tl, 2t, 16. Jose Luis Pelaez, Inc./Corbis: 4t. Martin Reeves/Eye Ubiquitous: 22. David Scarf/SPL: 18c. Ralf Schultheiss/Picture Press/Corbis: 14. SPL: 19. Andrew Syred/SPL: fr cover b, 3b, 10. Visioars/AKG London: 24.

Whilst every attempt has been made to clear copyright should there be any inadvertent omission please apply in the first instance to the publisher regarding rectification.